MARRIED TO PTSD

BY

S. Laguer

&

T. Hedgepeth

Table of Contents

DEDICATION

We affectionately dedicate this book to anyone who is coping with PTSD.

1

[11] www.iamstephania.com

www.tiarahedgepeth.com

The Lord bless you and keep you; the Lord make his face to shine upon you and be gracious to you; the Lord lift up his countenance upon you and give you peace.-
Numbers 6:24-26 ESV

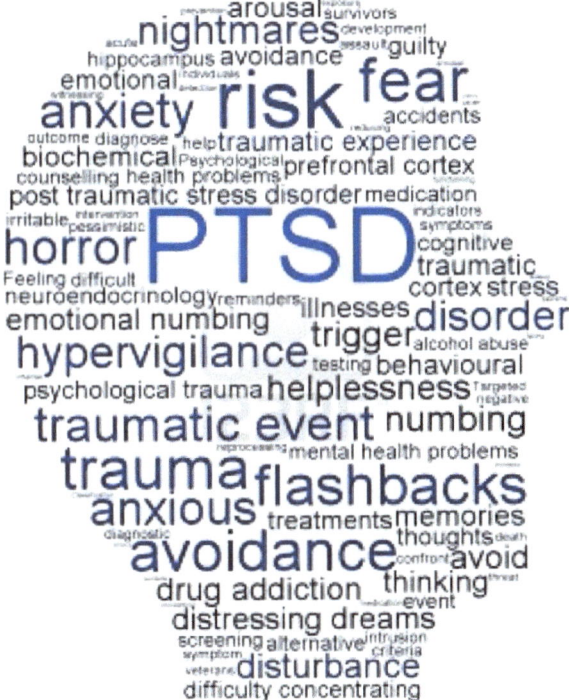

2

Do you know what it's like to have a type of deep pain that doctors and medicine can't cure? Welcome to our world of PTSD (Post Traumatic Stress Disorder).An estimated 70 percent of adults in the United States have experienced a traumatic event at least once in their lives, and up to 20 percent of these people go on to develop Posttraumatic Stress Disorder, or PTSD.

[2] www.iamstephania.com

www.tiarahedgepeth.com

Natalie & Stephen

Loving you …..…

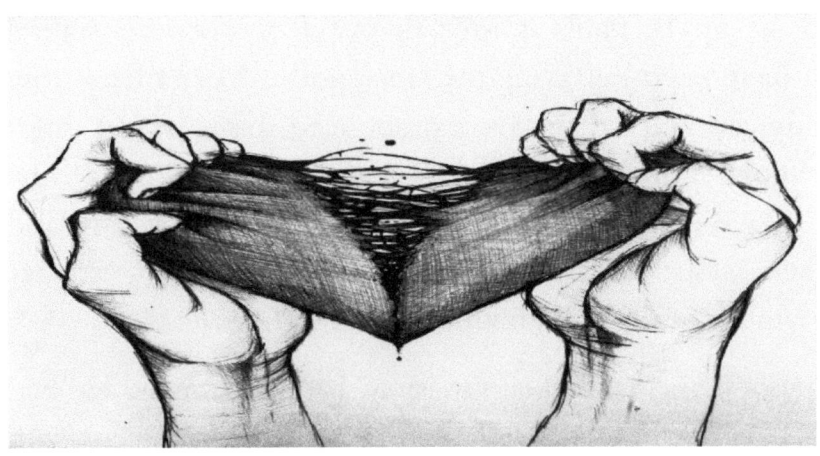

It's so natural to prejudge somebody without knowing anything about them. You never comprehend what somebody is experiencing or have experienced. I'm regularly reprimanded for leaving my marriage. Yet, truth is nobody knows what I experienced. My decisions are my decisions and I implored on every one of them. I walk by confidence not by sight. I did what was best for my children. It all came to an end when I woke up in a profound sweat from a repeating bad dream I can't shake. The bad dream is of a man chasing me with a blade that I can't seem to escape.

As I glance at the time on my alarm clock I see a shadow standing over me and talking softly saying "You don't love me no more" I jumped up and seen Stephen (my husband). I asked Stephen "what do you mean?" Before I could sit up he hauls a firearm out from behind stating "You have been betraying my trust, and if I can't have you, nobody can Natalie" I have experienced this a billion times in the course of the most recent year and it has gotten to be numb to the inclination of trepidation. See, my husband Stephen has PTSD which comes from Military deployments and early childhood neglect/abuse.

Stephen and I had been married for some years. He had been deployed twice, yet his PTSD originated from experiencing childhood in an unpleasant range of living from house to house. What my family don't or didn't know was I've been managing this horse crap for a few years. Never the less I was tired of Stephen and his suspicions and was no more in apprehension. I could have cared less on the off chance that he took my life as long as my children were alright. Our relationship had gotten to the point of no return and had become violent. We fought a lot, usually initiated by him. However I never let him just hit on me I retaliated and often got out of character. I was no saint but I definitely never initiated anything. Stephen started to become possessive, overly jealous and hard to deal with. As he changed daily, I changed as well. My verbiage and conversation with him became short and abrupt. Which usually started a fight. The PTSD was not just affecting him but it was affecting me too. I often reached out to his unit but received very minimal help. They seemed to be more concerned about Stephens's stellar job performance rather than his mental state. His command was very aware of what was going on, because he had received a DUI, assault charges, and weapon violation outside of work hours off of the base. Yet they still did nothing. This is more so why my sarcasm got stronger and stronger, I felt like I could only win by verbally sparring with him because clearly I was never going to win physically unless I put him 10 feet under.

Stephen and I have 2 boys conceived 11 months apart named Stephen Jr and Samuel. They are 3 and 4 and have had the terrible delight of being conceived in this wreckage. Let's be clear his condition had no effect on how awesome of a father he was, but I noticed his patience for the boys getting thinner and thinner. He dealt with our kids and constantly demonstrated love to them even when he didn't show himself or me any.

Stephen regularly debilitated to murder him or myself in the event that I ever left him.

So this was nothing out the conventional to me. As Stephen hauled the firearm out on me I started to guarantee him that I cherished him beyond all doubt and wasn't going anyplace. After around 20mins of asking and arguing, Stephen put the firearm down and started heading to the kitchen. I immediately heard him and shoot slugs into our rooftop. As he did that I was running from room to room trying to make sure my children were safe and gather their belongings. While putting my sons garments on I noticed the shooting halted and thought he may have return to his normal self which he frequently did. But of course I was wrong. As I walked to the door way, the front entry was clear so I continued to walk to my car and then the shooting began again however outside this time. I call the cops from my cellar phone however the area I live in the reception is bad. The only thing I could do was get in my car and leave for the wellbeing of my children, since my closest neighbor was a half a mile away.

I began to walk slowly and quietly to my car with Samuel in my arms and Stephen Jr holding my hand. Samuel was sleep so I encouraged Stephen Jr. to be calm and quiet. As I open the door to the car I look and Stephen was lying in the backseat and it appeared to be as though he was having a seizure, I went after my telephone again and was able dial out to 911. I disclosed to 911 what was going on and asked them to come quickly for the fact that I thought he was having a seizure. After I got off the telephone with them I saw Stephen quit moving. I put the children in the front seat and went towards the back to check his heartbeat and as I bent down he started strangling me saying "It's your fault I'm like this, you never loved me." Stephen says "I seen you talking with the postal worker down the road today for quite a while, you're going to leave me for him."

As I'm grasping for air I saw a look I've never seen in Stephens's eye it was an abhorrent look as though he was possessed. I promptly begin battling back and saying "I was speaking with him about your birthday gift I ordered." At this moment I understood Stephen was gone mentally and he was never returning. He was extremely gone in my eyes. Stephen had become paranoid, possessive and to a great degree desirous in the course of recent months. I mean he timed my daily movement, even my car mileage to the store since this was that was the only place I was allowed to go.

Everything we did was contend and battled; I was a detainee in my own home.

Do you know how it feels to live in apprehension? I dreaded leaving and dreaded remaining. I stayed in light of the fact that I knew it wasn't him and that it was his condition and I loved him. If I would have left, I would have feared for his life as well as anyone I interacted with. In any case, I never addressed Stephens where bout's or who he was with. I was really upbeat when he went out regularly to supply his needs mentally and physically. He had been undermining me this last year with numerous of affairs and I wasn't distraught in any way. Whenever he was out with other women it was less I needed to do sexually when he returned home. As awful as it may sound, I expressed gratitude toward God for the sideline ladies and managed it in light of his condition. However, the more he cheated the more away he pushed me. I even quit going to church, in fear that he would accusing me of cheating which he had done daily. I lost my self physically, mentally and spiritually. I simply needed my life back.

While Stephen was strangling me and my children were screaming, and he was yelling at them to be quiet (vulgarly). I couldn't help thinking that all of this was because I was speaking with the postal worker about a gift that I had gotten you. See with PTSD you just never realize what may push them; it could be the littlest thing. This is why I stated PTSD was like walking on egg shells. Since deal with a lot mentally, they frequently fear not being loved and dread their companion will abandon them. See over the course of the years what kept me solid was confidence and in a way because I knew this was not my husband acting like this. That it was this awful ailment that he had no one had influence over called PTSD. So I never gave up and kept upbeat contemplations and loved him in any case.

Please don't get it misconstrued, he wasn't generally this terrible mentally. Be that as it may, with PTSD, well Stephens PTSD it appeared like a Domino impact. When one thing happened wrong in his life and if he wasn't lifted up immediately, everything began to be negative. And his activities/ state of mind would reflect. The main thing that kept him normal was marijuana. I didn't agree with his habit, however I seen the distinction it made firsthand, I'd supported/added to his use. If he didn't have cannabis he was practically unequipped for anything. So I did whatever it took to keep my family rational and all together.

As insane as it sounds I cherished when Stephen was high because without it I felt like I was drowning. But when he was high I felt like I was coming up for a little air; and it was sufficiently enough to keep me alive. He turned into a delight to be around. We have attempted treatment in the past however it was not fruitful. He stated the counseling was stupid and made him angrier and I agreed.

Stephen was on meds yet infrequently took them because of how he felt while on them. He made statements that he felt dead on the meds, he said it made him think excessively.

Never ever would I have felt that me being the individual I am would endure such a great amount from a man or persist so much agony physically, and mentally? By now I had lost myself and was living for Stephen. I told my family/friends somewhat here and there however obviously individuals brushed me off and thought I was exaggerating. See NOONE will ever understand what you're going thru with PTSD or with a friend or family member with PTSD unless they go thru it themselves.

So I disengaged myself so I wouldn't need to hear the unneeded or judgmental comments from others. Particularly my family, they have a tendency to be old fashion and extremely demoralizing.

My name went from Natalie to BITCH, I was so use to this name at one point I pondered changing my genuine name to it. As I was battling him off the emergency vehicle and cops pulled up and he started punching me harder and harder and says you betrayed me you fucking BITCH, I abhor you and he spits on me. The cops attempted to stop him and as they were he then turns and spits on them as well. They then started to pursue him and got him on the ground and it took 3 of them.

Stephen wasn't going to stop. He kept fighting them, so they hit him with the crow bar and got him stagnant. They got some info from me and exhorted me to go get a restraining order in the morning.

Right then and there seeing him heading out and knowing he would be in care for a couple of days at least gave me so much peace. Peace I hadn't had in years.

I knew right then and there was no backtracking like I had done previously. I made up in my brain that I was divorcing PTSD yet remembering Stephen for the great times and not the terrible. See everybody just sees the peace yet they never see the war. I am currently a casualty of PTSD. I have friends that are not friends anymore they don't understand my choices. It's so natural to give somebody your feelings or considerations about their circumstance however it's significantly simpler to not need to experience their circumstance.

-For you, giving up doesn't always mean your weak, sometimes it means you are strong and smart enough to let go and move on.-

Andrea and Michael

I know I should throw the towel in but it's not that
easy.......

Is it ordinary to need to be with somebody physically yet mentally be with another person? Is it conceivable to be infatuated with 2 individuals for inverse reasons? Well my name is Andrea and I've been feeling like this for around a year. My spouse (Michael) and I have been hitched for a long time and after his last deployment he hasn't been the same. He's been diagnosed with PTSD. PTSD really means (Post, Traumatic, Stress, Syndrome); yet I allude to it as Pray/Trust/Smile/Darling. This tension issue is beginning to end up on a more regular basis.

It can happen after you encounter a traumatic event that include risk of harm or dying. I never comprehended what PTSD was and until Michael's condition. See for about 2 years he has taken me a passionate crazy ride. One moment "I cherish you", "I require you" then "I abhor you" or "I need a separation". Michael constantly recommended things would return as they were once he gets help; and his counseling was a moderate procedure. While adapting to his different emotional episodes, I began to practice my own therapy at the gym and framed different outlets as anxiety reliever. In spite of the fact that, we didn't have youngsters I'd frequently played the "mama roll"... ...

I heard a blast in the other room. "Michael, are alright", I inquired? He answered, "Definitely! Quit asking whether I'm fucking alright constantly!" I started again to PTSD (Pray, Trust, Smile, Dear). I attempted to release the frustration however he kept shouting. This is beginning to turn into a standard in our family? Michael says, "Stay away from me Andrea. I'm burnt out on you and I don't even know why I wedded you." At this time I choose to snatch my things and head to the gym. As I snatched my keys off the key holder, Michael grabbed them and said, "That is my car, my gas. You don't pay for shit. Walk!"

On the other hand, I've been unemployed 2.5 years out of the three years we've been married. Be that as it may, since Michael's new duty station, it's gotten harder to find work that would work around his appointments. Along these lines he turned into the sole supplier... ... As I went after the keys, he pushed me so hard to where I fell on the floor and landed on his dumbbell. I was so pissed; I snatched my sack and raged out of the house and walked three miles up the street to the rec center. I cried and petitioned God for clarity.

When I got to the base gym. I went to drink machine to get a water bottle before my workout. "Hey, are you alright?" This was a guy that I've seen at the gym before. I said, "Are you conversing with me?" He answered, "Yes and by the way my name is Vince. I see you all the time and you're generally alone. Are you married?" Normally I wouldn't go into subtle element with an outsider yet being that I was still pissed I answered, "Yes I'm married, however not happily." Vince glanced at me with a look of perplexity. So I started to walk off and begin my work out. When I returned home Michael was gone (he does this regularly, he stay's gone throughout the day and in some cases throughout the night.) However, I incline toward it like that in light of the fact that I'm settled when he's not around. By the by, this is the way it all began...... I proceed with my day by day schedules at the rec center same time regular and I begin to see Vince an ever increasing amount. We framed a perky companionship first

And foremost; however as time went on we started to talk about more individual things.

At the time I couldn't converse with my companions or family about what I was experiencing, on the grounds that everybody was living there own life and wouldn't get it. It's a great deal less demanding to convey what needs be entire generously to an outsider without being judged. See our discussions went from 15 minutes to an hour or more. This happened more than a couple of months. Vince turned into one of my new outlets. He didn't pass judgment on and gave incredible guidance; and here and there he simply tuned in. We traded numbers and even messaged every now and then. As Michael and I experienced stages, I started messaging Vince. He generally helped my circumstance.

One evening I choose to put a little zest back in our marriage. I googled a few thoughts and chose to have a sentimental supper; alongside an enticing move that I'd drilled throughout the day. I brought candles, wine, and a low light emission red underwear. Red was the shading he adored against my skin. I messaged Michael to see what time was he returning home and no reaction; obviously.

After I arranged the sustenance, I started getting dress and the telephone ringed. "Where the fuck is the cash" he said? I reacted, "What's wrong angel face?" "I'm attempting to purchase my fucking brew; the main thing that keeps me fucking normal, he answered?" I'm contemplating internally, no it doesn't it simply add to the issue. "There's cash in our record on the grounds that I simply utilized my card before, I said!" "You spent my cash bitch, he answered?" "I just burned through $50. It's well over $100 in the record, perhaps your utilizing the wrong stick, I expressed!"

Recently he tends to overlook things. He says, "You think I don't have a clue about my own particular fucking stick? Your fucking doltish I'm headed home." So I took a full breath and practiced my own particular PTSD. I sat on the love seat and waited......... Michael storms through the entryway and continues to shout, "Where's my cash?" I simply recollected that I'd actuated the new cards before and it programmed debilitates the old cards. I started to clarify what happened and apologized... ... I said, "I can go out and snatch your lager." Michael takes a gander at me and says," You're the dumbest young lady I know. I needn't bother with you to do anything for me! "I answered, "Would you like something to eat? I cooked your most loved meal" "I'm not in any case fucking hungry; I would prefer even not to associate with you.

So I propose you to call your folks and let them know you're getting back home, he hollered!" I chose to give him some space for the night. He said, "You better do what the fuck I said. Call your folks; truly get out at this point." I went to our room to put on sweats. Then, Michael keeps hollering and I could mind less what he's discussing. I'm simply attempting to get my stuff so I can go... ... I got in the auto and drove up the road. Acknowledging, I didn't have a spot to go, I stopped at the neighborhood supermarket. Incidentally, I get a content from Vince saying HRU? Ordinarily, I would message yet the way I was feeling I chose to call.

I clarified what happen and he recommended I come over his home until things cool off. I contemplated internally, this may not be a smart thought and after that reminded myself we're just companions. I instructed him to content me his location and I will be in route. As I pulled in Vince's carport, Michael messaged photos of my supper I cooked in the rubbish. I was hurt, embarrassed and baffled. I gaze upward and Vince is remaining by my entryway grinning. I couldn't do only grin back. As we go into the house it's similar to a genuine single men cushion.

Vince inquired as to whether I was hungry in light of the fact that he'd cooked. I didn't get an opportunity to have my own particular supper and I was starving. So I said, "Beyond any doubt. Give me a chance to see your aptitudes." He made my plate and presented to me some juice. He turned on the TV and that was exactly what I required. Somebody tend to me for a change, somebody to be there for me. I was agreeable and settled in his vicinity.

Michael did not enter my thoughts once. After my some juice I needed all the more however he was out, then again he had some Moscato. I thought, "What the damnation?" As we smashed our glasses and discussed positive things that one glasses transformed into another.

We snicker and talk throughout the night. I haven't had a night like this in a while. So we both laid on the sofa and watched parody motion pictures till we nodded off. In the "small" hours of the morning I alert to utilize the restroom; 5:30 am to be correct. This is my ordinary time to get up since I make Michaels breakfast each morning before work. As I was coming back to the lounge chair Vince got my hand and said come here.....I didn't delay, I just ran with it. As we laid there he kissed me delicately on my temple then on my nose. I felt each muscle in his body on mine. I ached for this. His hands started touching my back as his head laid near to my chest. I delicately kissed his head then he looked me in my eyes and we bolted lips. As we enthusiastically kissed my legs started to quiver I felt a vibe that I haven't felt in a while. He became aroused I wanted & needed it and he did to.

Renee and Luther

"At the time you tell yourself that being dead is better than having an incurable pain"

A considerable measure of you minded, sufficiently not (cited by Jay Asher). I'm certain that is the manner by which Luther was feeling before he took his own life. Why, Why, Why continues flowing through my head. On the off chance that I would have known the Extremities of PTSD, I would have asked more questions, pressed getting him help, conversed with someone about his issues, demonstrated to him more love. Damn, I would at any rate said Goodbye. My husband Luther was extremely depressed after his last deployment (8 months ago); he would dependably remove his self from Ryan (our 5 year old son) and me.

He wasn't affectionate or considerate any more. He would not like to communicate with Ryan. Before his last deployment he was extremely active with Ryan and exceptionally mindful to his needs. When he got back I expected everything was alright simply ordinary anxiety from a deployment. It typically takes him 1-3 months to change in accordance with life back home. However following 6 months I knew something wasn't correct. Also he barely ever rested and when he did he would wake up trembling in night sweats. He was always anxious, walking around the house watching out the windows as though somebody was after him.

He shut me out of his feelings and said "Renee you wouldn't get it. You don't even know me." I generally rebuttable, "I do know you." Renee simply back off please", he answered. I never pressed the issue of him conversing with somebody; in light of the fact that I myself like to manage things in my own particular manner at my own time. I did however address some of his colleagues wife's to perceive how their spouse were conforming. They all said their spouses were conforming fine.

Our marriage of 8 years got to be dull. As though we were flat mates. Ryan and I did a ton of things without anyone else excluding a few occasions. It was like Luther was soaking in a dark gap and he couldn't pull himself out. I knew he was discouraged however from what? I couldn't put my finger on it. He's been deployed four times and seen more causalities in prior deployments, so I thought. I did reach out on a few events to Military One Source. Military One Source gives military guiding, individual advising free of charge and it is classified. I even gave him the number.

However, obviously I was going about this the wrong way. I had no clue that Luther was so depressed he felt like his only outlet was to leave this world and his family behind. What will I tell Ryan when he gets older? By what method will I keep on living settled knowing I could have accomplished more? What's next???? That day everything began like typical. I got up with Luther to make his morning espresso. I generally ask him "How did you sleep" (despite the fact that if knew the answer, he didn't rest at all scarcely).

He generally answered, "I prefer to get some rest over none." I kissed him off to work and instructed him to have an anxiety free, gainful day. Luther would periodically get back home for lunch, so I would as a rule make his lunch and place it in the microwave before I take off for work. This day I overlooked in light of the fact that Ryan was giving me some major snags getting him prepared for school.

So around 11am, Luther typically goes to lunch, I messaged him, "Hey love, too bad I didn't have time to make your lunch, Ryan was in one of his inclinations at the beginning of today. There's lunch meat in the cooler." Not anticipating that he would respond because he ordinarily didn't. He said, "It's all good darling, I'm not hungry. Sorry for what I've been putting you through these last months. I know I haven't been myself. Ryan and you don't deserve that. Yawl deserve the absolute best. You have been nothing but the best our entire marriage.

I simply needed to let you know that. I cherish you! "I took a gander at my telephone and grinned. I messaged him back," I adore you". I just knew things were going to improve. I worked in sales and made eight sales after that message, and I was extremely amped up for going home. See our sentimental life has been dry these previous couple of months. We have had intercourse six times since he's been home. So, I was a bit excited and couldn't wait to return home and discharge some anxiety. Prior to his deployment we would have intercourse no less than 2-3 times each week.

I picked Ryan up from the after school project and he was exhausted. He nodded off in the car. I saw Luther's car in the yard and that was irregular in light of the fact that he seldom got in before me. I carried Ryan in the house to make sure he would stay sleep. I laid him in his bed. I began calling out for Luther yet got no response. I walked towards the carport to check whether he was out there however…..no Luther. I started walking towards the room and saw the washroom light was on and the door was broken.

I pushed open the door and nothing could have set me up for what I saw…….. Luther, my husband, companion, father of my child was dangling from the shower window rod with line tied around his neck… "Every man has his secret sorrows which the world knows not; and often times we call a man cold when he is only sad." -Henry Wadsworth Longfellow-

Nina and Jerry

"It's hard to wait around for something you know might never happen; buts it's harder to give up when you know it's everything you want."

It all began with that one telephone call.

I can't take this shit any longer. I'm done, he said!

At the time Jerry should have been at work for at least an hour and a half. Meanwhile, I'm sitting on the couch sipping my morning coffee and thinking he's just having another episode. He then begins to utter the words that no mom ever wants to hear, I forgot to drop the baby off at daycare.

My heart dropped. I felt as if I couldn't breathe. You know we all hear stories about people leaving babies in cars and it's usually deadly, so I was terrified. My first instinct was PLEASE tell me he's ok?? Although I couldn't get the words out of my mouth to even ask.
Meanwhile, in the background I over heard someone say.....Sir give me the baby! I'm not giving you my fucking baby, Jerry shouted!

Who is that, I asked? The MP's (military police), he responded! I grabbed my car keys by the front door and ran out the house barefooted. I began begging him to calm down. I pleaded for the sake of his son. I was terrified that his refusal to cooperate would put baby Nico in yet another dangerous situation. I knew Jerry was frustrated with himself. I could hear it in his voice. I just wanted to keep them both safe. I didn't want it to become more hostile than it already had. I could only think what everyone feels, "A policeman's job is to have suspects cooperate at all cost."

As I started the usual thirty minute drive that took twenty minutes this particular day, I probed into how this happened! He begins to explain that as he was working out in the gym and heard over the intercom that someone left their baby unattended in the car. The receptionist described the vehicle and demanded the owner to report to the desk immediately. Not realizing it was him, he shakes his head in disbelief and continues to work out. After his workout he explained he went to get a towel, located by the receptionist desk, and glanced out the front door.

 He then noticed his car was surrounding by MP's and regular pedestrians. He quickly ran out to see what was going on and saw Nico crying madly.
Ok Jerry, I need you to keep calm and I'll be there in a minute, I said! I got off the phone and immediately call Scott. Scott was his former company gunny (that's short for Gunnery Sergeant) and he's also a close friend. Living in

this life-style friends seem closer than blood relatives and they've been on a few deployments together.

 I knew that if anyone could calm the situation, other than myself, he could. Jerry trusts him.........
When I arrived Scott came over and said, "Please don't go in on him." Translation: Don't start arguing profusely because I'm known to have a temper.
I assured him that was the furthest thing on my mind at the moment.

 I just want my son! When I approached Jerry's truck he unlocked the door and handed over a smiling little boy. Nico appeared to be in good spirits despite all the commotion. My heart melted... a little but I was still on edge. I'm sorry Nina, Jerry said!
I walked back to my car I began thanking God for his mercy and grace. I've never been so grateful to smell the stench of baby vomit and drool.

I looked in Nico's big brown eyes and told him I loved him. It was if I gave birth to him all over again; instant joy and love. That's how I felt.
A policeman then approached me and began asking questions. Are you his mother? Are you willing to follow us to our headquarters for more questioning? I'm said to

myself, "Oh lord, I have to tell them what has been going on these past few months"..

You see, Jerry never wanted to talk to anyone in fear of his career being over and I could see it all spiraling down. Jerry loved his career and he was built for it. As a United States Marine and he enjoyed every minute serving his country. The MP's informed me of their knowledge of his PTSD. I assumed Scott exposed that because Jerry wouldn't talk to them. Anyway, these days he thinks everyone is his enemy.

The MP explained the reason he allowed Jerry to keep the baby was his genuine concern for the child. Although, I believe they would have had to physically take him out in order the get the child from him. Trust, he wouldn't allow anyone take baby Nico, regardless his mistake, he was very protective.

Jerry then stepped out the vehicle and walked toward the MP's. He was placed in the back seat and taken to the station.

While at headquarters we were introduce to the Criminal Investigation Division (CID). We walked down a long hall with offices along both sides. Jerry and I were then split up. He was two doors down from Nico and me.

A man walked in the office as I was sitting there. I quickly stood up......Hello, I'm Mr. McKnight, he stated! He explained he was a federal law enforcement agent and I politely extended my hand and stated my name as well.

He said, "Have a seat, let's get started. I know this has been an eventful morning so let us make this quick as possible." He flips through the papers he brought in with him and clears his throat......
Looking at the notes, it states Jerry has PTSD and he has six deployments under his belt as well.....So how long have he been diagnosed?

I was thinking, say the minimum....Ummm, about two months. Who diagnosed him? He was seen by a Lieutenant; a military psychologist. What triggered this? Or did someone recommend he seek help, asked Mr. McKnight? I believe Jerry experienced a lot while deployed. He needed to get something off his chest.........Did you notice anything different?? I explained, Jerry wouldn't talk much about his experience of being deployed.

So where were you this morning, he asked? I was home getting ready for work and that's when I got the call. Would you mind if my partner and I came to your residence to assure it's a safe environment? I do mind..... My husband and I provide a safe and stable environment. May, I leave? Sure.......

Understand, only when hanging out with other families I would over hear deployment stories. The guys would reminisce about events. I believe Jerry was terrified that if he expressed his feels, it could possibly end his career. That's why he prolonged seeking help.

He is a grunt, a front-lineman built to fight. He loved deployments. He once told me Iraq was his home and that is where he belonged. Remind you, I'm home with our four year old son waiting for him..... Believe me, I felt as if I was walking on egg shells after each deployment. I never knew what to expect because he appeared different each time. It was a routine of adjustments ......new friends, attitudes, and issues on top of issues. [3]

Prior to deployments we had an easy relationship. We could talk about anything and now we do not discuss our day. I tried to engage Jerry in conversations in hopes of him expressing his feelings. And he would often say, the less you know, the better....... I'd ask, so why new friends? "New friends", he began to say, "Can't judge me and

3

I'm tired of people saying how much I've changed." Again, Jerry deployed six times. He was a part of the initial military action post 9-11 and his last two deployments were a little over a year.

I know he seen and experienced lots of action. But nothing could have prepared me for the events that would occur after this last deployment. The arguments and black-outs became weekly events. Along with some occasional car accidents. He became cold as ice and the more I'd ask the more frustrated he became. I'd just assumed the car accidents were due to intoxication; because Jerry was no stranger to the bar scene. He continued working extremely long hours. And often times, he left while I was asleep and returned late while I was asleep. Our oldest son barely saw him.

On a few occasions, he would text heading home and I wouldn't see him for two or three hours. Oh yeah, he would stop at a bar and wouldn't give me the courtesy of knowing his whereabouts. He told me he didn't have to call me and I don't need to check on him.
He was later diagnosed with TBI (Traumatic Brain Injury) which suggested the cause of "black-outs". I was once asked, "How could you NOT know what's going on with

your husband and you share the same home?" And that was just it, we shared a home.

Jerry's communication was almost nonexistent towards me. Eventually, his driving privileges were revoked on military installations due to his additional diagnosis. Soon after, he was placed on temporary retirement. He was in my face all day. I prayed for more time with my husband but not like this. I began to witness his "black-outs" first hand. He would yell my name as he came conscious and I would be standing in front of him. It was if he didn't recognize me. Jerry became angry and severely depressed. I felt his wrath daily. When I felt like I couldn't take no more, I would go to my closet and fall on my face. I know where my help come from.

I prayed and leaned on my faith in God. I vowed to never leave him. I can admit, at times I was scared but I loved him too much to leave. Jerry's diagnosis changed our family forever.

HELPFUL FACTS

Post-Traumatic Stress Disorder (PTSD) is a type of anxiety disorder. It can occur after you have gone through an extreme emotional trauma that involved the threat of injury or death.

Causes, incidence, and risk factors

Doctors do not know why traumatic events cause PTSD in some people but not in others. Your genes, emotions, and family setting may all play roles. Past emotional trauma may increase your risk of PTSD after a recent traumatic event.

With PTSD the body's response to a stressful event is changed. Normally, after the event the body recovers. The stress hormones and chemicals the body releases due to the stress go back to normal levels. For some reason in a person with PTSD the body keeps releasing the stress hormones and chemicals.

PTSD can occur at any age. It can occur after events such as:

Assault, Car accident, domestic abuse, Natural disasters, prison stay, Rape, terrorism and War.

Symptoms

There are three types of PTSD symptoms:

1. RELIVING THE EVENT, WHICH DISTURBS DAY-TO-DAY ACTIVITY

   - Flashback episodes in which the event seems to be happening again and again

   - Repeated upsetting memories of the event Repeated nightmares of the event

   - Strong, uncomfortable reactions to situations that remind you of the event

2. AVOIDANCE

   - Emotional numbing or feeling as though you do not care about anything

   - Feeling detached

   - Not able to remember important parts of the event not interested in normal activities

   - Showing less of your moods

   - Avoiding places, people, or thoughts that remind you of the event

   - Feeling like you have no future

3. HYPER AROUSAL

- Always scanning your surroundings for signs of danger (hyper vigilance)

- Not able to concentrate

Startling easily

Feeling irritable or having outbursts of anger Trouble falling or staying asleep

You may feel guilty about the event, including survivor guilt.

You may also have symptoms of anxiety, stress, and tension: Agitation or excitability Dizziness, Fainting, Feeling your heart beat in your chest, Headache

Signs and tests

Your health care provider may ask how long you have had symptoms. PTSD is diagnosed when you have had symptoms for at least 30 days.

Your health care provider may also do a mental health exam, physical exam, and blood tests. These are done to look for other illnesses that are similar to PTSD.

4

TREATMENT

Treatment for PTSD involves talk therapy (counseling), medicines, or both.

TALK THERAPY

During talk therapy, you talk with mental health professionals, such as psychiatrists or therapists, in a calm and accepting setting. They can help you manage your PTSD symptoms.

They will also guide you as you work through your feelings about the trauma.

There are many types of talk therapy. One type that is often used for PTSD is called desensitization. During therapy, you are encouraged to remember the traumatic event and express your feelings about it. Over time, memories of the event become less frightening.

During talk therapy you may also learn ways to relax, especially when you start to have flashbacks.

MEDICINES

---

[4] www.iamstephania.com

www.tiarahedgepeth.com

Your provider may suggest that you take medicines. They can help ease your depression or anxiety. They can also help you sleep better. Medicines need time to work. Do not stop taking them or change the amount (dosage) you take without talking to your provider. Ask your provider about possible side effects and what to do if you experience them.

Support Groups

Support groups, where people who have similar experiences with PTSD, can be helpful. Ask your provider about groups in your area.

Expectations (prognosis)

PTSD can be treated. You can increase the chance of a good outcome:

- See a health care provider right away if you think you have PTSD.

- Take an active part in your treatment and follow your provider's instructions.

- Accept support from others.

- Take care of your health. Exercise and eat healthy foods. Do not drink alcohol or use recreational d⁵r ugs. These can make your PTSD worse.

Although, traumatic events can cause distress, not all feelings of distress are symptoms of PTSD. Talk about your feelings with friends and relatives. If your symptoms do not improve soon or are making you very upset, contact your health care provider.

Seek help right away if:

You feel overwhelmed

You are thinking of hurting yourself or anyone else

You are unable to control your behavior

Last longer than three months

Cause you great distress

Disrupt your work or home life

---

[5] [5] www.iamstephania.com

www.tiarahedgepeth.com

References

Bisson J, Andrew M. Psychological treatment of post-traumatic stress disorder (PTSD). Cochrane Database System Rev. 2007 ;(3):CD003388. [PubMed]

Gilbertson MW, Orr SP, Rauch SL, Pitman RK. Trauma and posttraumatic stress disorder. In: Stern TA, Rosenbaum JF, Fava M, Biederman J, Rauch SL, eds. Massachusetts General Hospital Comprehensive Clinical Psychiatry. 1st ed. Philadelphia, PA: Elsevier Mosby; 2008:chap 34.

Hetrick SE, Purcell R, Garner B, Parslow B. Combined pharmacotherapy and psychological therapies for post- traumatic stress disorder (PTSD). Cochrane Database System Rev. 2010 ;(7):CD007316. [PubMed]

Roberts NP, Kitchiner NJ, Kenardy J, Bisson JI. Early psychological interventions to treat acute traumatic stress symptoms. Cochrane Database Syst Rev. 2010;(3):CD007944. [PubMed]

Review Date: 3/8/2013.

Reviewed by: Fred K. Berger, MD, Addiction and Forensic Psychiatrist, Scripps Memorial Hospital, La Jolla, California. Also reviewed by A.D.A.M. Health Solutions, Ebix, Inc., Editorial Team:[6] David Zieve, MD, MHA, Bethann Black,

---

[6] www.iamstephania.com www.tiarahedgepeth.com

www.ingramcontent.com/pod-product-compliance
Lightning Source LLC
Chambersburg PA
CBHW050841290526
45792CB00001B/485